The Educational Pyramid of Success

By
Richard A. Jones, II

PublishAmerica
Baltimore

© 2007 by Richard A. Jones, II.
All rights reserved. No part of this book may be reproduced, stored in a retrieval system or transmitted in any form or by any means without the prior written permission of the publishers, except by a reviewer who may quote brief passages in a review to be printed in a newspaper, magazine or journal.

First printing

At the specific preference of the author, PublishAmerica allowed this work to remain exactly as the author intended, verbatim, without editorial input.

ISBN: 1-4241-7209-8
PUBLISHED BY PUBLISHAMERICA, LLLP
www.publishamerica.com
Baltimore

Printed in the United States of America

Dedication

This book is dedicated to my parents, my family and all those who are involved in education in the United States of America. It is especially dedicated to all the students, faculty and staff at River Valley High School. And to my wife; without all her encouragement this would not have been written.

Table of Contents

Introduction 7

Chapter One: The CPR's for Success: Commitment, Passion and Respect 13

Chapter Two: Positive Mental Attitude 25

Chapter Three: Find a Wise and Positive Mentor 29

Chapter Four: Remember Those Who Influenced You 33

Chapter Five: Physical, Mental and Spiritual 39

Chapter Six: Never Stop Being a Student 45

Chapter Seven: The Educational Team 51

Chapter Eight: Students and Colleagues 57

Chapter Nine: Planning 63

Chapter Ten: Communicate, Communicate, Communicate 67

Chapter Eleven: A Professional Philosophy 71

Chapter Twelve: The First Three Days Rule the Year 77

Chapter Thirteen: The Top of the Pyramid 87

Conclusion 91

Introduction

I have enjoyed and still enjoy the classroom. I am much like a bee collecting pollen from a flower and I want to shed educational pollen wherever I go. I have been in the teaching profession over 32 years. I have retired from the classroom, but I have not retired from education. Who knows, in 10 or 15 years I may retire from the profession and art that I have prepared for and practiced. It would be a shame to take all the experience with me without sharing it with others. It seems to me that much of what I practice can be applied to many other professions, especially professions that deal with people. I have found that outside of one's faith and family, education is the single most important factor in determining an individual's success as an adult. If you care to, you can read the statistics that reveal a high school drop-out will earn $9,200.00 less a year than a high school graduate and that a college graduate or a graduate of an advanced program from a tech or trade school will make one million dollars more over their career than an individual with only a high school diploma.

I would like to include thoughts for teachers just entering the profession and those ready to retire. I am not an expert, but I am experienced. I have discovered that commitment, passion and respect are everything for any profession. Attitude often makes all the difference. Make sure you find and use a positive mentor. Stay away from negative people. Remember those who influenced your youth. Make and take time for yourself and your family. Never stop learning or trying new techniques to enable students to learn and be successful. Keep excited about what you are doing; if you are bored, you are boring. If the students are not your first priority, find another profession. Set your goals for the classroom and create steps to achieve those goals and write them down. Maintain good relations with and respect for your support staff. Discover what you believe in and be consistent. Your discipline should be firm but fair. Never forget that they are teenagers or children. Your greatest challenge may be your colleagues. Live up to your own standards, but do not expect anyone else to. Enjoy every day, it goes faster than you think. With all of this in mind, I would like to introduce you to the Educational Pyramid of Success. I read a book by John Wooden several years ago and he had a Pyramid of Success in his book. I have borrowed that concept and applied it to education.

Any Pyramid must have a solid foundation and this one begins with faith, followed by family and the educational team and then the principles by which you, as an educator, can make a difference in a student's life. Always remember that, as an educator, you are the single most important factor in the classroom when it comes to student achievement. Many in our profession would like to blame environmental or economic disadvantage for their student's lack of achievement. Or we may blame the parents or lack of parents for lack of success in our students. We must break this cycle of blame and put the responsibility squarely on our shoulders. If education in the United States is to improve to the point where it fulfills the needs of our most important resource, then we will have to be the driving force behind that improvement. We cannot blame government, school boards, parents or students. We must take the bull by the horns and enable our students to achieve.

Study the pyramid for a few minutes so you have it in mind as we talk. The base is our faith. Now you may not believe this, but we were all created with a God-shaped hole in our hearts. I thought this was my discovery, but my wife told me that Blaise Pascal came up with it several years ago. So as my pastor often says, "there is nothing new under the sun." In the Garden of Eden, God had fellowship with Adam and Eve and when they decided to eat of the fruit, they destroyed that fellowship and we have tried to regain the feeling and fellowship that they had. The only thing is we try to fill that God-shaped hole with anything but God; in doing so we do damage to ourselves and others. We seek all sorts of things, love, money, property, fame, you name it, and we try it. But we are made so that only one thing will fit and that is our love for God and His love for us. The Bible says we must love the Lord our God with all of our heart, soul, mind and strength and until we do, all our other loves will be in danger. This is true because nothing can fill the hole except God and we will become frustrated by all other things we try to stick in there.

Love the Lord with all of your heart, mind, soul and strength and your neighbor as yourself. This is a part of the base; we must love God with our heart (to love), mind (to learn) soul (to leave a legacy) and strength (to live), and our neighbor as ourselves. The thoughts in parenthesis are Franklin Covey's. We love God and then we love ourselves, not with a narcissist's love, in which we are always looking in a mirror admiring ourselves, but in the sense that we are made in the image of God and made to create and serve his purpose. It is not so much a pride as it is confidence in the fact that God made us and then equipped us to serve His purpose. So, it is a confidence, self-esteem and worthiness that supports the thought that we fill a gap that no one else can fill.

Your closest neighbor is your spouse, followed by your children, family, church family, co-workers and students. All of the teachings of Jesus apply to them. We often take them for granted and treat our closest neighbors rather carelessly.

The next section of the base is built on top of the foundation of God the Father, Son and Holy Spirit. And this includes: love, prayer, faith, hope, discipline and sacrifice. If you look at the outside of the pyramid you will find the words communication. It runs all around the bottom and along the sides. Communication is a recurring theme in the Educational Pyramid of Success. Without it the entire process dies. Love, prayer, faith, hope, discipline and sacrifice have to be communicated to everyone involved in the pyramid.

The education profession is not to be entered lightly. I was in my 3rd or 4th year of teaching and coaching football. The staff made a trip to Pittsburg to take part in a football clinic. The featured speaker was Paul "Bear" Bryant of the University of Alabama. One of the most successful coaches in college football, he did not share one single thought about offense or defense. He focused on the philosophy of coaching. He made a statement that I remember to this day, "If you can live without coaching football, do it." It takes a great deal of commitment to coach football or any sport for that matter. It requires all of your focus during the season and much of it during the off-season. Half-hearted coaches will end up being unsuccessful. The same can be said of teaching: if you can live without teaching, do it. As a teacher you will be asked to play several roles. You must be a scholar, disciplinarian and entertainer. You must balance the needs of your students with the demands of parents and the requirement of administrators. You should be able to do this with a smile on your face and joy in your heart. If you can do all this, then to paraphrase Rudyard Kipling, you may be a teacher. If so read on.

Chapter One
The CPR's for Success: Commitment, Passion and Respect

In order to succeed in any profession one must have commitment, passion and respect. This is especially true in education. Most people are equipped to develop skills they can use in a profession. One of the most important things to remember in a profession is that you should be able to find something you enjoy doing, be able to commit to doing it well and make a living at the same time. Many people wake up and head to a job they despise. If you are in education and cannot look forward to meeting with your students 8 out of 10 days, then change the conditions in your classroom so it is enjoyable or get out of the business.

Educating the youth of America takes commitment. This commitment is to the profession. In some ways it can be defined as professionalism. I often hear my fellow educators saying that they want to be treated as professionals, yet they may not act with professionalism. Education is a demanding business that goes beyond subject knowledge. Each school administration requires a teacher's attention beyond the classroom. Our contract calls for us to be in the building 15 minutes before our students. Many staff members are in the building thirty minutes, even an hour before students. However, others come in five to ten minutes before their class begins. They are in a hurry, often unorganized and undisciplined. Their class begins and they are not ready to engage the class or catch the attention of students. This cuts into education time and may lead to discipline problems in the classroom. Part of our commitment to the profession of education calls on us to live up to what has been asked of us. If we have duties before, during or after school we should be there at these stations on time ready to interact with students. If we are to be in position at 7:40am then we need to discipline ourselves to establish a morning routine that will enable us to be in position on time, ready to go; if you need an hour to get your face on and hair in place then do it early enough to be consistent in your arrival. I have some advantages here. My hair is gone and it doesn't take much time to conduct this part of the morning ritual. Get there on time.

If you are going to be professional you should dress professionally. I am truly sorry that someone came up with the dress down day. I do not want to dress as my students. While I am not calling for suits and skirts, I am saying we as a profession need to look sharp; for men, that may or may not require a tie. However, we should have enough of a commitment to the profession to be in clean, well fitting clothes and with our hair in place.

Don't wait to get to school to be mentally prepared for the day. Lesson plans do not have to be elaborate, but they should be written down a week in advance with enough instructions that any other teacher could come in off the street and teach the subject. Remember, plan your work and work your plan. This includes knowing that any equipment you may be using is in working order and ready to go. If you need audio-visual equipment from the media center then you should let the media center know at least three days before. Any film that you use in class should be previewed. Hand outs should be run off and ready a day in advance. We could go on with this line, but remember, most student discipline problems come about because we are not prepared to engage our students in meaningful learning activities. It is not easy to hold a student's attention in the classroom. Half hearted classroom preparation will often lead to a confrontation we do not need or disorganization that leads to student's dis-engagement.

Another part of professionalism is developing positive relationships with your colleagues. Teaching students requires the cooperation of every teacher in the building. That means supporting each other in a positive manner. The teaching staff must communicate with each other. I have noticed that when one teacher disagrees with the methods of another they often take their concerns to anyone but the teacher in question. This is gossip. Anytime you take a problem or complaint or a concern to anyone other then the person who could actually help solve the problem, complaint, or concern, you have become a gossip and are no closer to solving or settling the issue. Teachers are supposed to be able to communicate and often we never communicate with our fellow staff members. When a teacher is causing you some stress, go speak with that teacher first. Never, ever send a student or put a student in the middle of the controversy. Never talk about a fellow teacher in a negative way to your students or compare your class with their class. This may be the most unprofessional behavior a teacher can exhibit. Don't forget, students have the ability to discern this and will use it to put you in a compromising position. So, communicate with your colleagues first, then seek advice from your mentor or building administrator to help settle the issue. Now, this goes for talking about your building administrator, superintendent and board members. Stay away from turning your lunch period or planning period into pity parties. When you do this you are guilty of draining positive energy from everyone around you. Seeking advice and asking for help is one thing. A "pick a little-talk a little" session is another and reflects poorly on the profession. Only take problems to people who are in a position to help you solve them. In other words, take your concerns to those who can take care of your concerns.

My father-in-law often reminded me to ask three questions and then answer each in the affirmative before talking about another person. Is it good, is it true and would you want it said about you? If you can answer yes to each question; then you can say it. Misinformation and the lack of information can destroy an organization's positive spirit and unity. Too much information from the wrong person and not enough true information can lead to rumors and speculation. The problem comes when our imagination starts to think the worst about a situation and we allow it to harden into what we think is reality. This can be true for a district, school and the classroom. As educators that means we must keep administrators, parents, students and other teachers informed in a timely manner. We also ask the same from all those who are involved in the educational process. Remember, you must go to the source of the information and obtain the information for yourself.

THE EDUCATIONAL PYRAMID OF SUCCESS

Do not believe everything you hear in the teacher's lounge. Often your colleagues are sharing an opinion rather than true information. They may not know the difference and you may not be able to tell the difference. Even if you hear it, you can break the rumor cycle by keeping the information to yourself and then forgetting it. If we are to be treated as professionals, we must stop spreading rumors about our students, their parents, our administrators and each other until or unless we can answer the three questions in the affirmative. You see, the educational process is a team effort that operates along a triangle. At the peak is the student; at the base are parents and the educational staff, and positive, informative communication must be maintained all along the points of the triangle.

My dad once told me to choose a subject, fill up on your subject and then let God pour it out. Now he was a preacher and was speaking of the method he used to prepare and deliver his messages. He was passionate about his subject all of the time. If you plan on becoming a successful teacher, you must be passionate about your subject.

I have been in a classroom in September since I was five years old. Most professional educators have been on one side of the desk or the other since they attended kindergarten. In that time I developed a passion for the specific subject of history. I have found great delight in wading through primary and secondary sources and various points of view, organizing them, and then developing a presentation for the classroom. Once the preparation is finished I pour the information all over my students. The secret lies in finding various methods in order to pour the information on your students. I started out teaching the way I had been taught. I was a sage on the stage and lecture was the primary method of presenting information. There is nothing wrong with a good lecture on a historical topic. The problem comes when the person giving the lecture delivers it right from the textbook. We should give the students a little credit and the opportunity to read the text. Teachers should not lecture from the textbook. We should find another source of information and use it so that our students have another point of view. And we should always find good stories to weave into the lecture. New computer technology has opened unbelievable opportunities for history teachers to find other methods for teaching history besides the lecture. This also applies to most of the other subject areas, but we will discuss that later.

The teaching profession requires a life-long passion for learning. This includes your subject area and the profession of education as well. We always should be on the lookout for new methods and new research that enables us to understand how young people learn in the classroom. Many people believe that the summer is a vacation time for teachers, and there is no doubt that teachers need a time to de-pressurize. I often told my students that teachers were sent to the 'home' to be retooled for the fall. Few people realize that the summer is not only a time to re-energize our teaching batteries, but it is also a time to learn new material and new methods of presentation for the classroom.

I say this with all due respect for those who may have an MA in education, but unless you plan on teaching future teachers their methods courses, you may want to consider obtaining a graduate degree in your subject area. This allows you to fill up on your subject. Possibly, we should encourage the teaching colleges to develop an MA program that provides a balance between methods and subject matter. The initial granting of your undergraduate degree is just the beginning; your passion for your subject must drive you on to continued learning. Beware of teachers who brag that they have not changed their information or techniques for the past 25 years. That is much like being retired in place. All passionate teachers are continually gauging and examining their methods to discover what they need to do to perform at a higher level in the classroom. They are looking for new sources of information and better techniques for presenting their material to their students. The final test of your passion is the success of your students.

There are many ways to evaluate your classroom methods. One of the best is the National Board Certification process. I do not want to make an unpaid advertisement for the National Board, but if you want to test and discover your passion, classroom management, and subject knowledge, then the National Board process may be a challenge you want to tackle.

Your passion for your subject will carry over into your classroom. Often your passion will spark a similar passion in your students. We need to understand that students require a reason to take an interest in the classes we are teaching as well as responsibility for their education. The material that we present to our students must have some relevance for their lives. Passion for your subject can often reawaken your student's love for learning as your passion splashes over onto them.

For reasons beyond our discussion at this point, many students have had the spark of education driven out of them. The main reason for not going into it is the fact that I cannot do too much about what happens to a student before they arrive in my classroom. I have very little control over their circumstances outside of my classroom. However, I am able to control the way I react to the impact of those circumstances on my student's behavior and I can do my best to allow my students to see my passion and allow that passion to carry my students along in my wake. Remember, many of your students have been crushed by the circumstances of life. You may be the only passionate, positive experience of their day. Make sure you make the most of the opportunity.

Respect is one of the most important characteristics of a successful classroom teacher: unconditional respect for your students, parents and fellow educators. Most of us believe that respect is something that should be earned. As a matter of fact, do not expect to be given respect automatically. It is something you may have to earn. Let me be direct and honest: unconditional respect for students is the difference between the average and good to excellent teacher. Respect must be given before it can be earned. We have discussed the ways in which our respect can be demonstrated for our profession and our colleagues when we discussed passion and commitment. So let us focus on respect for our students.

As we model this characteristic for our students they will pick up on it, and in many cases will develop respect for you, their classmates, and themselves. I begin each of my classes in the fall with a frank admission of why I am in education as a classroom teacher. I inform them that they are the reason I am in education. I make sure they understand that if it were not for their presence in my classroom I would not be in the profession. If they were not in the classroom there would be no reason for me to be in the classroom. I attempt to welcome my students each and every day. I am glad to see them and I am pleased to see their smiling faces. I want them to know immediately that I respect them as human

THE EDUCATIONAL PYRAMID OF SUCCESS

beings and that it is my responsibility to help them reach their potential. Here is a key point. Each of my students and your students has a great deal of potential. Our responsibility is to help develop that potential and we must respect them because of their human potential. We may never know what our students will end up doing or being. We often end up pushing them to the next level and then we have to trust that our fellow educators will do their jobs at the next level.

I continue my opening day discourse by telling my students that I will do my best never to embarrass them in front of their peers. I also make sure that they know that there are three basic rules in my class; do be on time, do be prepared and do be respectful. This includes respect for me, their classmates and themselves. From this point I expand the discussion to define the characteristics of respect in my classroom. It means that they will listen when I speak and I will listen when they speak. It means that they will listen to each other without interruption. Respect includes the rule that we do not use words like stupid, dumb or retarded on others or to describe ourselves. I explain that a put down is a verbal cut that cannot be taken back and while we may question a person's opinion, we will not question a person's character.

I also spend some time discussing what it means to be prepared for my class. Sure, this includes all the common sense definitions of the term. Students need to read the textbook, although I have not read a good history textbook. Yet, a student must read to be prepared for class and class discussion. This inclucds bringing pencil and paper and any completed homework that has been assigned. I also attempt to remind them that they are to prepare their minds and have them open and cleared for action. However, this is another area that is often beyond my control. I have little or no idea what has taken place in their lives before they enter my classroom. A bad evening at home, at work or in a relationship can inhibit the intentions of your students to learn. Be mindful that these are adolescents and their moods change about every second and in most cases their inattention is not aimed at you, they just have a lot going on in their young lives. You may be a master at communication and still you will have to repeat yourself many times before all of your students hear what you are saying.

I am open about my family as well as my preparation, degrees and experience. I want my students to know that they are in good hands. I let them know about my passion for history and for education.

My respect for my students includes my attempt to treat my students the way I would have wanted my own children treated by their teachers. I will put forth the same effort to teach them as I would my own children. I remind my students of these thoughts all year, but especially during the first three days of school and first week of any semester. The first three days of the year rule the year. All procedures and practices must be presented and in place during the first three days of each semester and it would not hurt to bring them up from time to time and after vacations. It will save you a lot of trouble and heartache if you will establish the class basics over the first three days.

There is a reason for establishing respect as the foundation for my classes. I have discovered that students do not care how much you know, they do not care how skillful you are at presenting information, and they will not care for you or school until they know how much you care for them. If you are able to create a safe atmosphere in your classroom and help students to feel comfortable, accepted and loved, they will beat a path to your door, even if they do not care for your subject.

Chapter Two
Positive Mental Attitude

Attitude towards the profession is everything for a successful teacher. P.M.A. or positive mental attitude is necessary if you are going to be more than a good teacher. You must realize that you can do little about your circumstances. However, you can control how you react to your circumstances. When you walk into a classroom there are several things that you must consider in order to lower your stress level.

You have no responsibility and very little or no control over what has taken place in your student's lives when they're not in your classroom. We can check around and ask questions about our students and we should ask questions of our students and we should engage their parents. However, we do not know what has taken place at home, at work or even on their way to and from school. We know little about their environment away from school and little about their home life. Do they have two parents at home, a split home, are they living with guardians? How were they treated at home? Is it a positive atmosphere? Have they been beaten down mentally or physically? You see, you have no control over their circumstances and when students walk into your classroom, you will have to react to their circumstances. The student's age will also create the circumstances you will have to react to within a classroom. In many cases, adults do not behave as adults. Take care that you do not expect children and adolescents to behave like adults, as their brains are not yet fully developed. My experience has been limited to teenage students. Their moods change at the snap of a finger. I've learned not to take their comments or their actions too personally. If a student's action is a direct challenge to my authority, I will ask the student to step outside or ask them to remain after class for a little chat, as I have found that it is best to confront students privately. Then I asked them to explain their actions, and I will explain to them that I cannot allow their behavior to disrupt my class. In my class I try to use as many nonverbal gestures as possible to maintain discipline. It will have to be a matter of experience as to what method a teacher will use and at times the best reaction may be a raised eyebrow or a simple snap of the finger. Often a walk by the desk or a touch on the desk will do. Students will always test the line to discover if you really mean what you say. They are human, and they like the stability that they can find in a stable classroom where discipline is firm and fair. Knowing and understanding what you are able to control should help reduce stress and enable you to maintain a positive mental attitude.

The other side of attitude is a reflection of your own feelings toward the students in your class and toward the subject you teach, the profession you have chosen, and the staff you work with. Attitude is a difficult thing to hide from students and your attitude toward your

THE EDUCATIONAL PYRAMID OF SUCCESS

students will be reflected back on to you. The same can be said for our attitude toward our subject area profession. When we maintain a positive mental attitude toward our students, they pick up on the fact that we expect them to be successful. And they will detect that we are willing to do everything in our power to help them succeed.

I use note cards to discover a little about my students. On the first day I hand cards to the students and ask for their names, phone numbers and addresses, birthdates and email addresses. I also ask for the names of three students in class that they might be able to work with on group projects. I ask what grade they expect to receive and what they're willing to do to earn it. This gives me a little insight into what type of educational success they have had in school before they have become a part of my class. I also ask if there are any historical topics they would like to cover. The state tests often require specific coverage, but we still have some leeway in depth and method of coverage. It is appropriate to give our students some ownership in our classes. Students need practice in making good decisions, and while we cannot make them full partners we can give them decision making opportunities from time to time.

Here is another thought about attitude. Just like our students, we do have a life outside of the classroom. Sometimes we may enter our classroom after a difficult evening or morning, or possibly we have just had an unpleasant meeting with an administrator, parent or even a fellow teacher. This may be a challenge, but don't let what happens to you outside of the classroom motivate you to take it out on your students. You cannot control their circumstances. And they cannot control yours. They're not responsible for your circumstances outside the classroom. Do everything you can to maintain a positive mental attitude.

Chapter Three
Find a Wise and Positive Mentor

I interviewed for my first job five days before the school year started. I was hired Saturday before Labor Day and school began on Tuesday. I missed the new teacher orientation as well as the staff in-service, and I received a quick explanation of procedures on Tuesday morning before school started. My schedule that year included five junior American history classes. One of my classes was zero period, which meant that class began at 7:15 a.m. I had a couple of study hall duties in my day and it ended around 2:00 pm. All my student teaching had been in physical education, so that did not help much when it came to handling a regular classroom. I had a double major, so there was a base of knowledge for any of the social studies classes that I would be teaching. I spent the entire weekend writing notes for the first week. And I lectured as I had been lectured to in all of my classes since I was in junior high. Since I was hired so late in the summer, I did not have any coaching responsibilities. This gave me the time I needed to prepare for my classes. And I think it was an important lesson for me; don't overload new teachers with a lot of responsibilities. First year teachers have enough to think about without having to coach, serve as a class advisor and run the Student Council. First year teachers should know that it is ok to say no to a few of the requests the principal may make.

We did not have mentors for first-year teachers in 1976. I had to learn the ropes on my own. I had never used a 16 mm film projector before. So I learned how it worked and had to order films from the film center and it often took a week before they would arrive so I was forced to plan ahead. We did not have a copy machine and we did not have computers. Tests had to be typed by hand or written on a spirit master and then placed on a drum and clamped in place, soon inked copies would roll out. You couldn't correct mistakes on a master, and often the masters would wrinkle. I do not think I got more than 10 masters to copy without a wrinkle in my entire career. Most of the staff had purple hands on test days. I went through the first year without an official mentor; however two teachers took me under their wings and helped me with policy and procedures. I also found that if you asked questions most other teachers were willing to help. The secretaries were like mother hens and they looked after the young teachers and passed on advice. All these individuals are positive role models and good mentors. And I have maintained contact with one of my former mentors and often seek his help. It is important to remember that you should always keep the secretaries and the custodians happy. They are important people and will help make your life easier.

Today we have official mentors to help out first-year teachers. It is important that you find a positive mentor. A good positive mentor can be a person who will help you learn policy and procedures, they can also share which support staff members you need to know. They will help with equipment and copy machines. This is the easy part. In most cases a good mentor will help you with class management and presentation techniques. A good mentor will make suggestions, and above all, they will listen. There will be times when the educational profession can become frustrating, and even stressful. Usually this takes place when we are overwhelmed by all the responsibility or we feel that all of our efforts have resulted in little student progress or achievement. You should be able to express this frustration to a good mentor who will neither judge you nor share your frustrations with other teachers. A good mentor will keep everything confidential.

The other side of this coin is do not associate with negative people. Every profession has negative people who complain about everyone and everything. They have lost the joy of life, and if you hang around them, they will steal your joy as well. I have experienced this myself and to my deep chagrin I've been a part of it from time to time. One year we had a superintendent who for some unknown reason could not carry a conversation with people without making them angry. He just rubbed people the wrong way and the district was going through a financial crisis that required some of our staff members be laid off. All of this led to low staff morale and quite a bit of anger aimed at the superintendent. One afternoon after school, to let off a little steam, three of us decided to play a little golf. On a good day, I might be able to shoot 45 on nine holes, and we were having a good time. On the sixth or seventh hole we started to discuss the superintendent and our games went downhill along with our concentration and the joy of the occasion,

I think I sliced at least three balls into a nearby bean field. That helped me to learn a lesson: you cannot control your circumstances, you can only control how you react to your circumstances. Teachers can be as negative, critical, and as selfish as any people I know and every staff has a few who cannot help themselves and you cannot change them. All you can do is stay away from them. Do not hang around with them. Find a positive group of associates and spend a little time with them. Allow their positive attitude help you through the challenging times.

Chapter Four
Remember Those Who Influenced You

My teaching has been influenced by several people. I have been blessed by the fact that I had a solid base. My parents provided a stable home and established within me a certain set of moral standards that apply to life. This base was further enhanced by the fact that my wife came from a similar situation. This has led to a solid support foundation which has enabled me to focus on the education profession. I recall very few, if any times, where I left my wife in the morning and felt distracted by something that had taken place at home. This type of support made it possible for me to fix my full attention on my students while I was at school.

I am a composite of all the teachers I have ever had in life. This includes my mother and father all the way to my most recent graduate instructor. Consciously or sub-consciously I have retained the methods of those teachers that I found successful and have rejected those that I found unsatisfactory. Even though I have been influenced by all my teachers, I know that I have four teachers who have made more of an impact on my professional life than any others. I have developed characteristics that were passed on to me by all four. These four high school teachers had commitment, passion and respect.

Mr. Jim Miller served as my World History teacher when I was a sophomore at Mt. Gilead High School. He was one of the most knowledgeable men I knew. He never stopped preparing and learning. He dug up information all the time. From Mr. Miller I learned the importance of being prepared for class. I learned that you are never finished with your own education, because everything you discover can be passed on to your students.

Mr. John Quinn was my senior government teacher. When I was a senior the Vietnam War was on the news every night. Many of us were concerned about the draft and the war. We discussed these issues in government class. Most of my teachers used the lecture as their basic classroom instruction method. We took notes and then spit this information back to them on tests. While a good lecture can pass on a fair amount of information to a large group of people in a short period of time, they give little opportunity to develop opinions and even less opportunity to defend them. Mr. Quinn used lecture but he also forced his classes to develop opinions, take positions and defend them. He was the first teacher to expose me to simulations. A simulation places a student into the position of conducting research to develop a position and defend it or role play it. There are several types of simulations. Some place the student in historical situations and ask them to re-enact history, often with the possibility of reaching an alternative solution. Other simulations give students the opportunity to make policy and pass it on to decision makers. This was the type of simulation Mr. Quinn used. It was called "Hawks and Doves." It was a simulation of American foreign policy in Vietnam. One side was opposed to the US involvement in the war and the other was in favor. Each was trying to influence the president. It was an interesting process. We were forced to think on our own and develop policy that we could support with more than opinion. Mr. Quinn showed me that there were alternative methods to presenting information to a class. Each method had a purpose. In some cases the method used required some risk. Often it took the class out of its comfort zone. Most students were not accustomed to being asked to develop their own positions on issues. Lectures require very little development of evaluation and thinking skills. Students often react to this lack of familiarity with fear. So, it takes a very confident teacher; one confident in their own skills to take the risk and use new methods that will stretch their students as well as themselves. I learned from Mr. Quinn that is was necessary to use innovative teaching methods to enhance student skills. These methods force students to take their own risks. The students learned to make decisions and recommendations based on information available to them. These methods enable students to discover sources of information.

Mr. Paul Bremigan was my history teacher and my football coach. He always told me that being involved with students and players kept him young. Mr. Bremigan was an outstanding story teller. He had the ability to wrap all kinds of historical tales into his lectures. So much so, that he is one of the few history teachers who could often keep student's attention during a lecture. He once took a class into the lecture room. There was a rocking chair on the stage and he proceeded to tell us the story of Abraham Lincoln's assassination at Ford's Theater. The moment he got to the point where John Wilkes Booth shot the president, Mr. Bremigan pulled a track starter's pistol out of his pocket and pulled the trigger. Everyone in the room jumped a mile. We could not get away with that in today's environment, but at that time things were different and no one forgot the lecture. Mr. Bremigan could fill his lectures with all kinds of stories and diagrams. He would draw Dealey Plaza while lecturing on John Kennedy. He would go into great detail about the British three prong attack that led to the Battle of Saratoga. He had to have been well read to include stories in his lectures and be able to hold a student's attention with these extra bits of detail. He read all the time and usually read books on specific individuals and events. I never saw him read a general history book. To be able to develop interesting lectures you have to get away from the textbook. I never lecture out of the same textbook that my students can read. Why should I go over the exact same information that they can read on their own? My job is to expose them to as much new information as possible from as many different points of view as possible. Mr. Bremigan taught me the art of weaving a story into a lecture to hold student's attention. For example, the Gilded Age can be as dry a topic as a history teacher can attempt to lecture on. The Populists and their issues do not hold much interest for today's students. However, if you can use "The Wizard of Oz" and the analogies included in the book, the Gilded Age will take on more significance for the students. Once again, if students are not motivated or enticed beyond just learning for the sake of a grade we often fail at our task. Mr. Bremigan taught me that part of being a classroom teacher was to be an entertainer. History should be interesting, but we often destroy the subject for our students and that is a great shame.

THE EDUCATIONAL PYRAMID OF SUCCESS

Mr. Ron Thill was my biology teacher. He is still a good friend and advisor. We did leaf collections and a pig dissection. We even boiled a frog until the skin came off and then we re-constructed the skeleton. I spent one year at Mt. Gilead coaching the 9th grade basketball team and scouting for the varsity. Mr. Thill was coaching the juniors. One Friday night the head coach was down flat on his back with an injury and Mr. Thill and I coached both the JV team and the varsity. We were playing a very good team and they were taking it to us. He looked over at me and asked me what I thought we could do to get back in the game. We had tried everything including all the presses and defenses we knew. Mr. Thill did not have to involve me like that. But he always took the time to look after people and give them opportunities to be involved. But it was more than that; Mr. Thill had a genuine love for his students. Mr. Thill taught me that once students know that you care for them, it is easier for them to care about you and your subject. He did everything he could to help you improve as a student. But he went beyond that because he wanted you to improve as a person. He had a compassion for his students that I have seen in few other teachers. I think the subject he was teaching was often secondary to his care for his students. Mr. Thill taught me how important it is to treat my students with respect. He taught me to realize that every student is full of potential and that our job is not to put in more potential, our job is to pull that potential out of our students. It is often up to us to enable our students to discover that they have potential and a responsibility to use it to improve themselves and the world they live in.

Our classrooms would be more productive environments if we as teachers would learn to treat each student as a human being full of potential, with the ability to bring about change in their lives and in our world. Only then will we realize the great responsibility that teachers have. When I stand before my students and look at their faces I know they have potential, but I do not know where that potential may lead them. If I am not able to give them my best, they may not be prepared when the opportunity comes to use their potential to serve others.

The point of all this is that we often use teaching methods that were used by our teachers. We incorporate those techniques and make them our own. Look into the past and find those teachers who have most influenced you and use that to help you become a better classroom instructor.

Chapter Five
Physical, Mental and Spiritual

Of all the industrialized nations, workers in the United States take less vacation time than workers in any other country. No matter what the profession might be, people need to take some time for themselves and their families. This helps us to maintain balance as we move through life. We need to pay attention to three specific areas. These are the physical, the spiritual and the mental.

Many teachers are overweight, including me. This reflects the tendency of the rest of the nation toward corpulence. Teaching requires a lot of concentration and energy, energy we do not often have if we are out of shape. When I started teaching I weighed about 165 pounds and coaching kept me active. As time went on I became less active and began to gain weight. After my children graduated from high school, my activity level went way down and I became a couch potato. The winter months were the most inactive periods of my life. I returned home from school, snacked on my favorite type of chocolate and some kind of nut, and then I would sit in my easy chair and I would grade essays, watch TV or read. My physical condition was flabby to say the least. In March of 2003 I had a wake up call. About 2:00 in the morning I woke up with some pain in my chest. I took some antacids and an aspirin and went back to bed. I went to school, still in a little discomfort, and after school paid a visit to my doctor. By then the pain was more in my back than in my chest. My doctor sent me over for a few tests: an EKG, x-ray and a blood test. Then I went home and soaked in the hot-tub to relieve my back pain. Then the doctor called and informed me that the blood test indicated that I had had a heart attack and he wanted me back at the hospital ASAP so they could monitor me and then transport me down to Riverside Hospital in Columbus. Needless to say I was somewhat shocked by the news. An ambulance took me down to Columbus and since I was stable they decided to wait until the next morning to conduct the heart catheterization.

I did not sleep much that night and kept running things over in my mind. The biggest question was how did I let my body get into the shape it was in? I had done little to take care of it. I had become lazy when it came to my own body. The next morning the cardiologist came in and explained what would take place during the procedure. I was wheeled to the special room where the catheterization would take place. The cardiologist performing the procedure came in and was wearing a Cleveland Indians batting helmet on his head. He had it on backwards and was dressed in some type of protective gear. He got started and as he ran the catheter up my leg we talked about the American Civil War and its battles. That was right up my alley. But the best news came when he said, "Well this heart is as healthy as a horse." He said he could find no damage and that I had a little plaque build up in one of the arteries. When we finished he told me that my blood had sludged and that had caused my heart to spasm. I was lucky. They put me on some medication and sent me home. The entire event changed my physical life. I decided then and there that I would lose some weight and start to exercise. I walk and get in about 10,000 steps each day. That is about five miles. I walked the halls during my lunch period and also during time before and after school. I walked to the office several times each day and then walked at home. I used a treadmill for 30 to 40 minutes in order to force my heart rate up. Based on this experience I would make several recommendations to other teachers. Watch what you eat, do not take in calories in liquid form; don't allow inactivity to put you at risk and exercise. 30 minutes of exercise each day will help to reduce the stress that often comes with a day in the classroom. It also gives you a sense of accomplishment. I wear a step meter for motivation to walk. I cannot explain all the benefits of walking and exercise, but it has enabled me to have more energy and that made me more effective in the classroom.

While we are on this subject of fitness and diet, I might encourage you to drink all the water that you can. Do not walk past a drinking fountain without pausing for a drink. We all need to drink several more ounces of water each day than we do. One massage therapist told me to drink my weight in ounces each day. That is a lot of water, and of course, one of the side effects is that you get in several steps each day on the way to get rid of all the water you consumed.

I believe God has a purpose for everyone. My purpose is to be an educator. That is what I am equipped to do. This makes me no better or no worse than anyone else. Education just happens to be my calling. Other individuals are called to be electricians, doctors, lawyers, preachers, writers and mailmen. Some are to be farmers or work with computers or in communication. Since God has a purpose for each profession, there is no advantage to be in one over another. In that sense all are equal. Your spiritual side is very important. It helps to provide a base of operations, something or someone to lean on. I spend about 30 minutes each morning in prayer getting ready for the school day. My prayers are not the subject of this section. My point is that our spiritual side is a part of who we are. We need to nurture it to bring balance to life. My beliefs and my faith give stability to my life. It gives me a place of retreat, a compass for dealing with all sorts of challenges. I am not speaking of a specific church or doctrine; I am speaking of belief in and faith in God and developing a relationship with Him. In order to survive in any profession we need a foundation, a belief system to lean on. Mine is the Christian faith.

We also need to maintain mental health. The educational profession brings some stress with it. However, most professions have some form of stress. The key is to know how much stress actually goes along with any specific task. 90% of most stress is avoidable. Teachers must learn to say, "It's not my stress." Members of the teaching profession often take on stress that is unnecessary. There are events we are able to control and events we cannot control. In most cases we cannot control our circumstances; we can only control how we will react to those circumstances. We also tend to worry about events that may never take place. Our imagination is a wonderful tool. But we need to stop imagining problems that will never take place. Many of us build the bridge and then go to all of the trouble of carrying it to the river, only to discover that we can walk through the water and we never actually needed the bridge.

Education requires a great deal of mental activity and there must be periods of time when we give our minds a break. We must be prepared to exercise a little silence and solitude to get away from the routine and give our minds a chance to focus on nothing. There should be a time during the day when this takes place and it should be longer during the summer break or whenever a long break is scheduled. We need to schedule time for family, when we close the books and stop grading papers. We had a couple of practical jokers on our staff and, when they stay within the boundaries, they can provide plenty of humor and needed laughter.

Once the school year has ended it may require a few days to allow the routine to fade away. There must be a time when you push the teaching profession out of your mind. I get away from the area for a time and spend some time with my family. It has become more of a challenge now that my children are married and my wife and I are empty nesters. I find the empty nest to be very enjoyable and family gatherings are icing on the cake. Now that we have a granddaughter, I find that she fills the empty without refilling the nest. The point here is to maintain balance in your life to reduce stress and avoid teacher burnout. The education profession is very rewarding and it fills much of my life, but it is not my entire life.

Chapter Six
Never Stop Being a Student

I spent a day observing the operations of a large city school while on an in-service. The principal made it a point to inform me that he often changed the assignments of his staff within their areas of certification. His philosophy was that after four or five years of teaching the same subject a teacher could become stale. To make sure that his staff was always learning, planning, studying new materials and seeking new ways to present this information, he would rotate his staff into new assignments. Most schools do not do this. In most cases you are assigned to a specific area and may continue teaching in this area for quite some time. Usually, teaching assignments are based on seniority or interests. New teachers are often given the subject areas that no one else wants and they often are given the most challenging students. We may want to rethink this. A new teacher should be given a combination of classes that are a challenge, but that are not capable of overwhelming the novice teacher.

I have discovered that students are best served by those teachers who are passionate about their subjects and their student's achievements. While I understand what the principal was attempting to do, I believe that self-motivation is the best reason to continue to study and find new information and ways to present it. Many states now require a master's degree to remain in the profession. However, just because you have obtained a graduate degree does not relieve you of your responsibility to continue your education in your subject area. Now, I do not mean that you have to continue to take college courses. In many cases it can be an in-service in your subject area. It could be a study of a new book or exploring new technology. We have all heard the story of the college professor walking into class and pulling out a set of lecture notes that had turned yellow over time. Educators must avoid this temptation to rest on our past accomplishments. We must be tireless in out effort to find sources of information and research it, then pass it on to our students. We need to continually be aware of the new methods of presentation. Have you ever sat back and imagined the perfect classroom for your subject? Several years ago when computer technology was being made available to teachers I imagined a computer based social studies classroom with computer stations for each student along with printer and scanner all connected to the Internet through a high speed connection, a classroom without walls and without textbooks. When I retired I had the classroom of my dreams.

I created a new class called Interactive Social Studies. It was an online based research and presentation class. We participated in online simulations such as the ICONS negotiation simulation sponsored by the University of Maryland found at http://

www.icons.umd.edu/ and we joined Learning Circles established by I*EARN found at http://www.iearn.org/. We conducted all kinds of research on the net and used presentation methods from PowerPoint to the more conventional poster board projects. Now, this happened to be the way I engaged students in this particular class. It was unconventional in many ways, but my students learned how to use the computer for more than downloading music and instant messaging. They became researchers and like good researchers took their presentation responsibilities seriously. My challenge was that technology was growing so fast that I was always behind the curve. My next imaginary classroom will be based on holographic technology that will be programmed to transport students into any historical event and enable them to interact with historical figures and be actual participants in the event. I know, it will take a great deal of money and the technology had not been developed yet, but give it some time and this classroom will be a reality, just as soon as technology catches up with my imagination. What do you want your classroom to look like? What do you want your students to accomplish?

This brings us to the thought of developing an individual mission statement for your life and your class as well as personal goals and classroom goals. Proverbs says, "Without a vision, the people perish." You must know where you are going in order to know that you have arrived. My mission statement is to "Learn all that I can in order to teach all that I can to those that I can in every way that I can as long as I can." That is a lot of cans, but it is important to focus on your mission and your goals. There are many ways to go about writing a mission statement and setting goals for your life and classroom. One of the best can be found at http://

www.franklincovey.com/fc/library_and_resources. I am not going to walk you through the process of developing your own mission statement. Franklin Covey has many resources available for you to accomplish that on your own. You should realize that to develop a mission statement is to focus your life and it is a good idea for your students as well.

You can establish classroom goals and mission statements or you can engage your students and allow them to aid you in developing these. Remember, for a goal to be effective it must be written down and it must be measurable. By doing this you have a method for holding yourself accountable and will be able to discover if you have met all your goals for the year, you will be able to determine where you have fallen short and you can plan new methods for achieving the goals you or your class may have missed.

People who write their goals on paper have a tendency to reach those goals and in doing so are successful. Once you record your goals, write down the steps you will take to achieve those goals and when you plan to achieve those goals. For example, let us say that I want to lose 20 pounds. I write down the goal is to lose 20 pounds, I am going to do this by walking 2 miles each day and not eating ice cream and I am going to accomplish this by June. I have a written measurable goal with an action plan and a target date for reaching the goal. I share my classroom goals with my students as well as the action steps. I post the goals in the room so all are able to see them.

All of this helps you to keep from being bored with what you are doing. There is no reason for students to be bored in class. If you are bored with what you are doing, your students are bored with what you are doing. Continue to find new methods to refresh yourself and your class. Exploration of new information or points of view as well as methods of presentation can bring new excitement to the most experienced educator.

Chapter Seven
The Educational Team

During my years in the classroom I was blessed by being associated with outstanding administrators and board members. Now, don't get me wrong, there were times when we went head to head over some issues, but we always came away from the encounter with understanding and respect. We did our best to operate as a team. The educational team includes everyone involved in the educational process from parents to superintendents. The team includes custodians, bus drivers, cooks, secretaries, teachers, administrators, aides, and all the support staff. The team is to work effectively at producing results, in our case, students that are well prepared for the next step in their educational process. Too often we look at administrators and boards as adversaries and that should not be the case. One way to accomplish this is to always deal with each other with respect.

All new teachers should become acquainted with the secretaries, custodians and cooks in their buildings. These individuals can be of great help to any teacher, but especially to the new teacher.

Let me give you an example of how the educational team should operate. One year our superintendent came to the high school staff and said, "I want to revitalize the high school." I did not know exactly what he meant. I think it was his way of saying that we were in a rut and we needed to try some new methods and that we should come up with them. He was wise enough to understand that is it difficult to impose change from the top down and that most effective change comes from the bottom up. He told us to go out and explore, the board would provide the resources and monitor progress. The high school staff spent four years researching options that included technology, different types of schedules and various methods of instruction. We sent teams to visit other schools that had made successful changes. We met and shared all the information that we had accumulated and we discussed and debated all of the possibilities. Then we voted on a specific plan and held two overnight retreats to design our reorganization. The staff voted to focus on the 4x4 ninety minute block schedule and all that would be required to make the change to extended period instruction. Once we decided on the block schedule, the visitation process began all over again. We visited schools and began the process of examining everything we did and why we did it. We studied our discipline policies, the number of minutes needed for passing time, the number of credits needed for graduation and even our field trip policy. We had to discuss parent-teacher conferences and when to hold them as well as interim reports. In point of fact, there was little that we did not debate and discuss. At the conclusion of the four years the staff had developed a unity of purpose that has been difficult to recreate. We presented our findings and recommendations to the board and they approved our adoption of the block schedule; then came the hard part of implementing the block in our individual classrooms and all the adjustments that would be required. The entire study had re-energized the staff and we found ourselves working together for a common purpose. This is just one example of what can take place when the staff, administration and the school board work together for the common purpose of improving student achievement. We do not have to be adversaries, we do not have to be in competition, and we need to function as a team.

The issue here is respect for the educational team. This begins with the superintendent and the board of education. I know there are times when it may difficult for you to do this. I have been associated with education long enough to know that not all board members are qualified to hold their positions. Most board members are very good willed people and take their responsibilities seriously. However, some board members do not respect teachers nor do they understand the education process. When this takes place you need to educate them and earn their respect. Board members are in a difficult position. They have to balance the needs of the school district with the concerns of parents and the desires of administrators and teachers. Add to that equation that the state has mandated many rules and laws and often does not fund them. So the superintendent and the board are forced in directions they may not want to go, but the state calls the shots. I have found that the majority of board members that I have been associated with were highly motivated by their concerns for the community and the education of students. I respect them a great deal for their sacrifice of time and energy as they do a tough job with little pay or public recognition.

The same can be said for administrators. I had some outstanding building principals and assistant principals as well as very good superintendents. They have a real challenge in trying to balance the needs and wants of students, parents, board members and staff. In a fully functioning school district the superintendent and principals are much like referees. If they do their jobs right, you never know they are there. In some cases they can become lightning rods for every pet peeve in the district. When in leadership positions we only have so many quarters of influence to spend. Sooner or later you use up all those quarters and your effectiveness as a leader will come to an end. Most quarters are spent on controversial issues. Some superintendents have the ability to spend their quarters in a judicious manner; others seem to spend them very quickly and are not with the district very long. I would not be an administrator for all the money in the world. There are too many balls to juggle. You have to keep too many groups happy in a general sense. And as President Lincoln said, "You can please some of the people some of the time, you can please some of the people all the time, but you cannot please all the people all of the time." It takes an outstanding leader to balance the needs of teachers, parents, students, board members, administrators and community members. Our principal seemed to be putting out so many fires that he had little time for the academic side of his job. So, since I would not be in the position of an administrator, they have my deepest respect for all that they do.

While we are on the subject of the educational team, let's discuss the unsung heroes of the educational system. The non-certificated staff makes the largest impact on my day outside of my students.

They are the individuals who make sure that my room is clean, the halls are waxed and they deliver my students safely to the building. They serve hot lunches at mid-day and keep the bathrooms clean. You may not understand this or realize it for some time, but the secretaries run the building. Many of us assume that the building principal is in charge. However, if you want to learn how to operate a copy machine or remove a paper jam, the secretary is the person to ask. Often they are the only people who actually know what is going on. The support staff is as important as the superintendent and the board when it comes to the successful education of our students. We are a team and the team works together for success. There has to be respect for every member of the team. Maintain good relations with the non-certificated staff, they can be the greatest supporters we have.

Chapter Eight
Students and Colleagues

What is your first priority as a professional educator? Your first priority should be your students. Most days it will involve preparation and presentation in your subject area in ways that help you to focus on student achievement. Other days it may be helping students get into a position to be able to learn. By that, I mean you may have to teach students how to learn, you may have to learn how students learn and you may be required to teach your students how to study. If students are not your first priority, then you may want to consider finding a different profession. Let us face the facts, students are the only reason the education profession exists. Our jobs only have purpose as long as students are in our classrooms. I make a point of telling my students that if they were not in the classroom, I would not be in the classroom. Many teachers believe they work for the superintendent or the school board or parents. Do not get me wrong, all of those people serve as a part of the educational team. However, we serve our students and their need to be prepared for the next step or level that they will soon move toward. In business terms, our students and their achievement is the product we produce. Everything we do in the classroom should revolve around their success. Now, you may think that I am over simplifying here. But students should be our first and only priority. How could it be any other way? If there were no students there would be no need for teachers.

We have to take care that we never allow ourselves to forget the reasons we entered the profession. The longer we stay in education the more tempting it becomes to stay in a rut and find the easy way to accomplish our responsibilities. We continue to resist change and decide that we have always done it this way so we will continue to do it our way. It reminds me of the story of why mom always cut the end off of the ham before putting it in the oven. When asked, she said that was the way her mother always did it. So we asked grandma and she said the same thing. We moved on the great grandma and she told us that she always did it so the ham would fit in the pan. Today the stoves are bigger and so is the pan so there was no need to cut off the ends, but that is the way we always do it. Our excuse for not making changes in education or our classroom should never be, "Because that is the way we always did it." We must be aware of new methods and explore them without fear. We should not make excuses: my father often told me, "An excuse is the skin of a reason, stuffed with a lie."

When we make students our top priority we should be able to avoid the pitfalls that trip up many educators, no matter how long they have been in the profession. For example, if we make students our top priority we will not allow our conversations in the teacher's lounge to be about students and their shortcomings. We will stop complaining about them and their parents and come to an understanding that we are the single most important factor in the classroom when it comes to student achievement. When students are our first priority we stop complaining about the conditions in the building and search together for solutions. When we make students our first priority we will stop complaining about in-service.

Let us address in-service opportunities. I have had many in-service opportunities in the over 30 years that I have been a professional educator. I believe if I add all the time I have spent in in-service it may equal a semester. Some in-services have been entertaining, funny, challenging, and outstanding as well as thought provoking. Other opportunities have been down right mind numbing and spirit breaking. I wish I had an answer on in-service. We went through a string of in-services where the topic changed like the weather and we were never given a chance to put any specific topics we learned into practice. Once we had a two part in-service and the presenter gave us the same information both times. Let me tell you, we were not a bunch of happy campers that day. A one size fits all in-service may not be possible, but many administrators are heading in that direction. It is my belief that the best in-service is one that meets the needs of students and teachers. If you find yourself in an outstanding in-service, be grateful and make the most of it. When you find yourself in the mind numbing in-service, there is only one thing you can do. Concentrate and find at least one thing that you can take with you from the in-service. This is better than joining the negative complaining that will take place. Let's get back to our first priority, students.

When students are our first priority we will not talk about other staff members in a negative way in the teacher's lounge, we will not stab them in the back, or talk about them with our students in a negative way. When students are our first priority we will not barbeque the principal, board or superintendent in our classroom. Nor will we compare other classes to ours in a negative way. You see, when I do any of these things I am attempting to lift myself up in the eyes of someone else at the expense of someone else. It puts students and colleagues in the position of having to take sides with you and they may have to side with your judgments and opinions. When students hear teachers talking about other teachers or students they will usually go and inform that teacher or student about the content of the conversation. This often causes a rift and may cost the offender the respect of colleagues and students.

Now, you may ask what you should do if a fellow teacher comes to you to share some information about a teacher, student or administrator. There is a major point to be made here. The point is this: individuals should take their concerns to those who can take care of their concerns. I have this underlined because it is a most important principle. If you are a part of the concern or may be able to share some advice as to how to take care of their concerns, then by all means share your information. If the material does not involve you in any way then you should inform the person that you do not participate in that type of activity. If you are comfortable in your skin you might tell them that you would rather not talk about the issue or a person you have no control over. Then suggest that they take it up with the person in question or the administrator in question. If you feel that you might offend the teacher sharing the information, you might try to change the subject. For example, I had an individual start to go negative on a colleague, so I asked the individual about the price of corn. It was off topic and it told the offender that I would not participate in the conversation if it were to continue in a negative vein. Whatever method you use, you can stop the chain or at least let people know that you will not be a part of that activity. I employ this principle in my classroom as well. I will not allow my students to speak of other teachers, administrators or students in class. That is something I share with them on the first day and in most cases I have to remind the students of this throughout the year. I tell them that it is not appropriate and in most cases they are talking to the wrong person. There are some things I just cannot control, so I suggest they discuss the matter with the guidance counselor, administrator or person in question. You need to develop some discernment here. I had a student come in with black eyes and I asked him what had happened and he told me his dad had hit him. Well that is another matter all together and we had to deal with it. The first stop was the guidance counselor and then the situation took its course from there.

Chapter Nine
Planning

"Plan your work, and work your plan." I have heard this statement so many times I am not sure who to give credit for it. The first time I heard it I was in at a football clinic in Pittsburg and Bear Bryan of Alabama was speaking about the coaching profession. The statement is very simple yet it is very profound. Everything you do in the classroom must have a purpose. You only have so much time to share the material you have prepared for your presentation, so you have a great responsibility to plan everything well. In the movie *Gettysburg* General Lee tells General Longstreet to plan it well, meaning the attack on the 3rd day at Gettysburg. He was staking everything on the attack. Parents and students are resting much of their future on how well we plan our activities for the classroom on any given day. Why do you do things the way you do in the classroom? What is your purpose? Why use one technique over another? How do you introduce a new topic? Why and when do you use an assessment tool? What type of assessment should you use in a given situation? Does the assessment reflect a state mandated model? How do you design your lessons? How much and what type of homework do you assign and why? How do you make sure that the students understand your instructions? Is it busy work? Does it have meaning? What do the grades in your classroom represent? Should you give extra credit? What is the rationale for all that you do in the classroom? Do you use a seating chart? How much multimedia should you employ in the classroom? It is time for a lecture, a PowerPoint or a student directed activity? Did you preview the film? Why use a film? What are your goals and objectives for each lesson? How do you know when your lesson is effective? Do they reflect the state standards? How do you plan to use the assessments for future planning? There are many more questions that we could ask. This is why we need to plan and the bottom line is student learning.

People often asked me what I was doing during the summer now that school was over for the year. I told them that I was preparing for my new classes that would begin in the fall. The reply that I usually received was one of doubt; they could not believe that I was preparing for school during the summer. I use the summer for depressurizing, renewal and retooling. I told my students that the administration would usually send us to a "home" for teachers so that we could be treated for our conditions, you know, all those nervous tics. So the summer is for rest and relaxation, but it is also a time to refocus on the profession and to prepare for the fall. By the end of July I begin to establish a general set of goals and objectives for each class. I review the lessons I used and improve and recreate old lessons so that they will be more effective in the future. I throw out lessons that did not work and I create new lessons. I work in the summer to create a schedule of use for the lessons and to make sure they line up with the state model curriculum. I read all the new material that I can find on American and European history. I spend time surfing the Internet searching for web sites that may be useful for my Internet based classes. There are thousands of lesson plans on line that can be used in all subject areas and you can revise them as needed to fit the specific needs of your class. Summer planning makes it possible for me to focus on individual student needs during the school year. It also reduces the stress and pressure since I have most of the general work in place. I realize that the best laid plans of mice and men can go wrong so be prepared to make adjustments as the school year develops. Your specific class planning should include the principle of having at least one more activity for your class during a class period. I have found that being over prepared and leaving little free time for your students helps to avoid quite a few discipline problems.

Do your students ask you what you are doing that day, or are we doing anything important today or can we have a free day? You can avoid these questions by communicating the following thoughts to your students. We do not have time for a free day. All of our days are planned out, so students know we do not have the time for a free day. All that we do in this class is of importance to my student's learning and we do no busy work and I explain to my students the importance of everything we do. I explain each step and we discuss why it is relevant to their success. I also put the day's activities on the board so there are no questions as to what we are doing in class that day and the order in which we are doing it. My students are able to come into my room, check the board and prepare for what is to come. I also prepare a syllabus for each of my classes that outline the schedule we plan to follow. I want to keep my students as informed as possible so that they are able to focus and their knowledge of our activities provides security.

Most students are not secure dealing with the unknown so keep them informed. I also post test watches and test warnings. These are similar to weather watches and warnings. A watch means that the conditions are favorable for a test. A watch is posted when we have covered a certain amount of material and I am satisfied that my students know the material. A warning means that the test has been constructed and its distribution is imminent. A test is an assessment tool and can be used in several ways. It will demonstrate my student's knowledge and skills in a specific area, for example, it may test their writing and study skills. A test will demonstrate how successful my presentation methods have been. If several of my students have difficulty on the same question or questions, the assessment enables me to ascertain the weak point of the presentation and make adjustments. I should ask a few questions to make sure of the problem. Once I know the reason for my student's lack of understanding, I will develop a remedy that will address the problem or the weakness. All of us need to use the assessment as a tool to help us plan future instruction. An assessment should never be used as a discipline tool. Do not give a quiz or a test just because your students have made you angry and you want to get revenge. An assessment is to demonstrate student achievement and a teacher's skills at presenting information.

Chapter Ten
Communicate, Communicate, Communicate

All along the outside of the Educational Pyramid of Success runs lines of communication. We must be able to successfully communicate with our students, their parents and our colleagues and administrators. When communication breaks down all kinds of things can happen and many of them are not good. We need to keep everyone informed along the lines of communication. This is a two way street. The entire educational team must practice outstanding communication skills. It's not like we do not have the necessary tools. We have our own speaking abilities, email, phones of all types, regular mail, computer programs that can supply information from homework to grades, and written memos carried by hand to the home or office, and our feet for face to face communication.

Keep parents informed as much as possible. You will be able to avoid a lot of hassle by initiating communication with parents. Let's say you have to give a parent some bad news about their child's grade. There is a way to do this. When you call with the news about grades you might ask the parent to help you and suggest some positive alternatives so that the student will improve. In many cases the parent will come looking for help and suggestions from you. Do not allow bad news to build up to the point that it is too late for the parent or student to do anything about it.

If direct communication does not take place, many members of the team may develop their own conclusions. If the conclusions are wrong and they spread, it may lead to perception and that perception may become reality. When people begin to speculate they often draw the wrong conclusions and accept their own conclusions as reality and pass it on. In that case speculation can often become gossip. This gossip hardens into a position that must be defended and that may force team members to take sides which divide the team. A team divided against itself cannot provide a quality education to students. The team's focus has shifted from the students and their achievements to some issue or other members of the team. The issue often deals with some type of right that someone else may be taking away, or it may have to do with money or added duties or some type of threat that may or may not exist. I have witnessed a lot of sweat expended over a threat that never developed. All the individual had to do was ask the right person the right question. Here is what may take place. The superintendent and the board have their interpretation of the contract and the teachers have their interpretation of the contract. Each assumes the other understands these interpretations and all go on their merry way until one or both stumble over an issue. This happens all the time. We all have different interpretations of the same event. If we are willing to take the time to explain our positions to each other we could save a lot of time and effort. However, we often wait until each side has backed itself into a corner with undue speculation and it splits the team; whereas, all of this could have been avoided with direct and open communication in a timely manner.

There are keys to knowing when communication has started to break down. The most visible takes place when one part of the team begins to see the development of a conspiracy. Someone will start to talk about being a target or we might refer to others as 'they', it is always they, but I have never been able to figure out who they are. Are they going to force us to do something or give up something? I have yet to find a single good willed administrator or board member who was out to do anything but ensure a good education for the students of the district. We must be careful not to allow our imaginations to cause division. Most disagreements are over how to accomplish a goal rather than the goal itself. The point is that you should seek out the source of the information and find out for yourself. Take your concerns to the person who is able to take care of your concerns. In some cases it may be another teacher, in other instances it will be a parent or administrator.

I will make the case for positive mental attitude at this point. I worked one summer for the county highway department mowing roadsides and patching potholes. I met a man who had worked for the county for several years. He told me a story that I have never forgotten. He told me that one of his friends broke his arm in several places. Then he told me that he advised his friend to stay out of those places. There are times when the teacher's lounge can be a negative place. I would advise you to stay out of that place and do not take part in it. Negative attitudes can spread and they will sap a teacher and an organization of its strength.

Chapter Eleven
A Professional Philosophy

What do you believe in and why? What is your educational foundation? What is your philosophy of life? During the 1992 Vice-Presidential debates one candidate, Admiral James Stockdale, who was running with Ross Perot, was somewhat unknown. He was a naval aviator and had been shot down and taken as a POW during the Vietnam War. The majority of those watching had little idea of what to make of Admiral Stockdale. So during the introductions he asked two questions about himself, "Who am I? Why am I here?" If you are able to answer these two questions you are well on your way to developing a philosophy of life and a philosophy of education.

In many cases a philosophy will develop over time before it becomes a solid foundation. It goes without saying that you have to stand for something or you will fall for everything. A philosophy is not a goal. A philosophy is a belief and a purpose. Who are you and why are you here? I ask this question of my World History students when we study the Enlightenment and the philosophers. I receive answers that run from the well thought out to the selfish. In many cases they give me their reason for being and reason for living. Without a philosophy an individual will wander through life aimlessly and without purpose a life may be wasted. As we go through our lives as students and educators we need to take stock of our values and what we hope to accomplish. This will help us to develop answers to the question of who I am and why I am here. When I was an undergraduate student I had the privilege of sitting through several methods classes. The professor was always talking about developing a philosophy of education and he encouraged each of us to develop one of our own. I had no idea what my philosophy was and he went on to tell us that we need to write one on paper because prospective employers would be sure to ask us for our educational philosophy. I have been through the interview process a few times and I never had a superintendent ask me about my philosophy of education. I am not sure you can develop a philosophy of education until you have been in the profession for a few years. You might be able to work on one as an undergraduate and then revise it as you become aware of the realities of the profession.

My philosophy has matured over the years. At this point I would state it in this way. I was created for God's purpose and pleasure. It serves His purpose and pleasure for me to be in the education profession. I believe that every child has the ability to learn. I have been equipped to do all that I am able to do to enable my students to learn. I cannot control my circumstances, but I am able to control my reaction to those circumstances. To the best of my ability I will not allow my circumstances to become stressful. This is a general philosophy; the details have developed over the years as I have developed my skills and explored the various methods a teacher has at their disposal to reach students. Therefore, the bottom line does not change. The academic development as well as the social development of my students is my prime responsibility. However, the means to accomplish this responsibility may change. All teachers must realize that one size does not fit all in the classroom. At times a majority of the class with respond to a well designed lecture. At other times it will require a multimedia presentation or a student directed assignment. What you are willing to do for those who struggle will often determine your quality as an educator.

Do not get me wrong. I know that all students are able to learn, but not all students will learn at the same rate. There are many factors for this. But one of the most important is the fact that you cannot control what impacts a student outside of your classroom. Life has taken many of the students we will encounter and has beaten them into the ground so much that they do not see the importance of their own education. We can rail against society and parents and the environment, but we are accountable. We are the single most important factor in the educational success of our students. This must permeate our teaching. We must not look for others to blame when a student fails. We must look for solutions in every area to enable them.

Yet, you may run into a student who will not respond to any efforts you make to help them achieve. The bottom line is that all students need to be held accountable for their own learning. This may be one of the tough areas of education. I cannot learn it for them. There will be students who will not want to be held accountable for their lack of success. There are good choices and there are bad choices, but it still comes down to the choice of the students.

I attempt to make it possible my students to be successful. It is not always easy. In many cases I ask them just what it is that they want. So we have to establish some level of trust and determine what it is they can do and are willing to do. It usually will begin with some small step of success. We may start by completing a reading assignment or a homework assignment. Sometimes I gather a few who are behind in their reading or are not completing assignments and we work together and I model how to complete an assignment. In many cases our students do not have the necessary skills to do what we ask. I may have to establish the fact that they are able to do what I am asking so they are confident and ready to move on to more difficult material. Many of our students have never seen themselves as successful so it is easier for them not to try rather than to try and fail again. Often they have the ability, but for some reason their confidence has been driven out of them. Many students need to experience some success in education or in life in general in order to develop some confidence. When I find myself in a situation such as this, in regards to a student, I often turn to the philosophy of Machiavelli. I am willing to do just about anything to make sure a student has a little success. I want them to demonstrate to themselves that they are able to accomplish what I am asking of them.

There is a line I will not cross. I will not do it for them. They have to be accountable for their success and learning as well as their lack of learning. School should not be a place where young people come and watch old people work. It is a place where learning takes place and young people are doing most of the work. There may be times when it is tempting to give up on a student; at that point we should remember all those individuals who made sure we were successful. So we renew our efforts and seek out others for ideas and methods to reach the student. Always take the opportunity to pick the brains of master teachers who have been through the battles that take place in education. Many times they have solutions to our problems and challenges.

Sometimes circumstances will take a student beyond our realm of influence. The grading period ends or the semester or school years ends and the student has not reached the level of academic success that is required or they have given up. I was working with a student who was very intelligent, but was operating in a home environment that worked against him and he had made some poor choices early in the year. Just at the time he was turning away from the "dark side" he made another poor choice and was expelled. He moved on to another school system and out of my influence. I had to let him go and trust that he would not be allowed to fall through the cracks of the educational system. If he had remained in my building we would have been able to continue our relationship and at least visit with each other while he changed classes. I could have spoken to him as he moved through the halls. Maybe some other teacher had the opportunity to build off what I had started. Teaching is one field where you may never know of the impact you had on an individual's life and success.

Chapter Twelve
The First Three Days Rule the Year

We had an outstanding assistant principal for several years in my building. He had been through the ranks as a classroom teacher, building principal, superintendent and then back to assistant principal. I think our principal talked him into coming out of retirement to help us out. He had well over 30 years in the profession and his philosophy of discipline was to be firm, but fair. Building and classroom discipline can be a challenge. Students today are exposed to much more in the way of information technology and the source of the information is always at their fingertips. This has changed some of the dynamics when it comes to discipline, but in many ways teenagers and children have not changed. They still want boundaries and they want acceptance and they want to fit it. They will challenge the boundaries because they are seeking independence and looking for their identification. We need to learn to respond to their challenges in a non-defensive manner. We need to inform them as to why the boundaries are in place and provide a rationale for their existence.

Building and classroom discipline is a matter of team work. Much of the building discipline is set by the administration and board of education and their policies. These include attendance policies as well as tardiness, clothing, language, hall traffic and that sort of stuff. If a policy is on the books it should be enforced or it should not be a policy. The building principal usually has his or her hands full making sure that the teaching staff is consistent when in comes to policy. Some staff members have an eagle eye for the smallest infraction, others wear blinders. My suggestion is to follow building policy and enforce it to the best of your ability. Classroom discipline must be the responsibility of the classroom teacher.

The first three days of the year rule the year when it comes to establishing a well ordered classroom. This is the time to present classroom policy and procedures, including discipline. These must be accomplished to ensure student success. So, what are the principles of discipline in your classroom? Allow me to share with you what I do during the first three days of school. I put all of this material together as a handout and a PowerPoint presentation and I have many of the procedures hanging on the walls of my classroom.

My basic discipline is called the "Do Bees." Do be on time, do be prepared and do be respectful. Then I add a final thought; don't do anything I don't like. These are somewhat general in nature, but each of the Do Bees has a specific idea to them. As I have said, I discuss these over and over the first three days. And I remind each class of the Do Bees every Monday for a few weeks. I use Do Bees because I want the discipline to be positive in nature, I do not want to nag on the negatives so I focus on a positive theme. Then I explain the rationale behind each Do Bee. There is a reason for all that we do and I want my students to understand the reason behind the activities that we conduct. When a student asks why, I explain in as much detail as possible. "Because I said so," is not a good answer, especially for teens. However, I also let them know that there are times when, "No" is a complete one word sentence.

DO BE ON TIME: This may be the easiest to explain and the hardest to maintain in a consistent manner. Since the institution of the factory system our society has been tied to the time clock. In many ways it is a shame. We seem to run here and there to maintain someone's schedule. It is the culture we are a part of and since most of us will work for someone else, we are required to be at a certain place at a certain time. Our employers will expect us to be on time. So, it becomes a matter of self discipline and it should be instilled in our young people. When you are on time you create a sense of trust with the people you work with and for. They have set a part of their day for you at a certain time, they want to know that they are able to count on you to be there to accomplish what you need to accomplish. When we become disciplined in the small things the large items take care of themselves. It is a matter of respect for others and their time. Teachers should model this discipline by being in class on time, returning graded assignments in a timely manner and being at staff meetings on time. If you are going to require your students to toe the line, then you should model the behavior for them.

I believe the school policy was 3 tardies before any discipline was to take place. Here is what would happen. A student would be tardy twice and have no excuse, and then the 3rd tardy would take place due to some unforeseen event such as an accident blocking traffic. The principal would have to explain to the student that they were given three tardies for such types of events, and they used two due to their own lack of organization or they decided to sleep in. It never ceases to amaze me how we humans will play the system for all its worth and then complain when we were burned by our own decisions. We had an attendance policy that gave students 8 unexcused absences during a semester, the 9th unexcused absence called for failure of the class. It did not happen often, but from time to time a student would use all 8 and then they got caught on the rule because of some event that was totally out of their control. Good choice, bad choice, your choice.

DO BE PREPARED: Being prepared for class may mean different things to different teachers according to the specific subject they might be teaching. In a physical education class it may mean having gym shoes, in a technology class it may mean having a laptop, in my class it mean having something to write on and write with. It also included completing the reading assignment and being prepared for class discussion. In my Interactive class it meant having met the requirements for a presentation project and being in the class to make the presentation. In an Advanced Placement class, preparation might require reading a section of the textbook several times and taking notes for class discussion or being prepared to write a document based essay or an open essay in class without notes. This preparation must become an expectation and it motivates students to develop the needed skills over and above those they may have.

Over time the students will come to understand what it takes to be prepared for a specific class. I do not have the time to allow my students to come and go to their lockers for pens, paper and pencils, so I keep a healthy supply of all these materials in the room. Some students like to play the game of going to their lockers for materials and then they roam the hall as I tend to forget about them and go on with the day's lessons. So, why fight this battle, I charge them a few points and supply the material and we move on.

If we are going to require that our students are prepared for class then we need to model the behavior by being prepared for class. I know there are times when last minute situations or unexpected situations may come up. A bulb may go out in the overhead or the Internet connection may fail. We need to have a backup plan in place when technology fails us. However, this does not happen very often and we need to have handouts, tests, movies, and technology ready to go. Remember we tend to bring discipline problems on ourselves when we leave an open time within the class. We need to fill the educational time with education. I do not appreciate it when someone wastes my time so I do my best to make sure that I do not waste the time of my students. Return homework in a reasonable time period. We should expect no more of our students that we expect from ourselves.

DO BE RESPECTFUL: This is the cornerstone of all that I do in the classroom and is the basis for success in much that I do. I respect others because they were created in the image of God. I am compelled to respect His handiwork. This respect starts with my respect for myself and then I am able to respect others. This is a point to be made and remembered. The Golden Rule works only when you love and respect yourself. If we are willing to misuse our bodies and our lives then we will be willing to misuse others. Students and adults are often abusive to others because they abuse themselves. They have little respect for others because they have little or no respect for themselves. In many of our students this self-respect has been demolished by family or circumstances of life. We may have to rebuild it. It may also provide some understanding of why our students behave the way they do.

I make it a point to inform my students that they have my utmost respect and I tell them why. I tell them that I see in each of them a great deal of potential and one of my responsibilities is to help them to achieve that potential. If I fail them it will leave a void in our society that someone else will have to fill. I do not expect their respect for me to be automatic; I will have to earn it. I hope to earn it during our time together, however I do demand that they respect my position as a teacher and my authority. This means that when I speak they listen and I will listen when they speak. I expect them to listen to each other and explain to them that all opinions are welcome, especially those that they can back without emotion. If you have to get violent to defend a position, you have no position to defend.

Now that we have the idea of respect in place in the classroom, many of the other standards of discipline will fall into place quite naturally. We treat each other with respect. We do not put others down to pull ourselves up. We have a society that just loves to put labels on us. I do not allow character assassinations to take place in my classroom; we do not use terms like, idiot, moron, stupid or words such as those. It is all right to disagree with each other without adding some type of adjective to the discussion. It is okay to debate ideas; it is not okay to debate each other's character. Many of my students like to make a cutting comment and then say that they did not mean it. Well, that does not cut it. Once the words are out they have accomplished the purpose that the speaker had in mind. The damage has been done and you cannot take the words back or heal the wounds that they cause. So the principle becomes, think it, but don't speak it, better yet, do not even think it. I have informed my classes that it is a sign of maturity to have an idea pop up in your mind and not have it come out of your mouth.

Once again, it is we teachers who must model this behavior in class in front of our students. To gain respect we must give respect. We cannot belittle our students in class; we cannot use demeaning words to our students and expect them to perform. We must set high standards for our own behavior before we attempt to raise the standards of our students. We must take care not to set standards for our students that we are unwilling to live up to ourselves.

DON"T DO ANYTHING I DON'T LIKE: I know this is a very general statement, so I make sure that my students know, by the end of the first 3 days, what it is I do not like. Let me share a few things that I do not like to take place in my classroom. I do not like my students to use profanity or vulgarity. I explain to them that educated individuals should not use questionable language to communicate. This is the place where I decide to use a little humor to keep the discipline positive. "Don't cuss, call Gus, Gus will cuss for all of us." If a student slips and uses language I do not like, I do not jump down their throat. I just remind them that we do not use that type of language in my classroom and tell them to call Gus, his number is BR549. Another phrase I do not care for is, "This sucks." I tell my students that, little babies suck, black holes suck and vacuums suck, but what we are doing does not suck. Eventually my students come to an understanding of the forms of language that I do not appreciate them using in my classroom.

I do not like when my students write on their desks. So I inform my students that I will provide paper or PostItNotes for them to use. They can write on the note and leave it for the next student and that student will be able to read it and respond. I do not like it when students remove other student's materials from their desks. I do not like it when they pick on each other verbally or physically. I tell all my students these facts during the first three days and remind them so there is no misunderstanding.

I use a seating chart and have it in place for the first day. I tape the names of my students on the desks so that they are able to find their place before our first class begins. In this way I do not have to take the time to move students around on the first day. I can take attendance quickly and learn their names at the same time. I do not use a seating chart for discipline, I use it because it takes me time to memorize all my student's names and the chart helps me to put faces and names together. I have to work hard during the first two weeks to accomplish the task. I hand back all their homework papers during this time to help me establish their names in my mind. I may have to revise the seating chart as I become acquainted with the character of my students. I also give them an opportunity to change seats from time to time. I do not align my desks in the usual manner, in rows front to back. I have my desks set in rows that face each other. Each row is three desks deep and there are five rows on each side. When the room is organized in this fashion I am able to change the front of the room easily and no student is less than 3 desks away from the front or middle of the room. This may not work for everyone, but it works for me.

Here is another point. The teacher's desk is to be used for paper work. I find that the teacher's desk acts as a divider between the teacher and their students. So when you are in the active mode of teaching stay with the students and do not teach seated at your desk. You need to be at the board or moving among your students. When I give a lecture on a certain historical topic I move among the desks talking and making sure students keep their attention on me. It is a simple discipline tool, but it may save you a lot of work when working with your students. It helps you to stay on top of things.

By asking my students to find their seats as they arrive I begin to establish the sense of discipline that is expected in my class. Once attendance is taken, I go one through the opening day routine and use the PowerPoint to present my Do Bees and other policies and practices for the class. If a textbook is to be used I have it on top of the desk for them and have the number recorded along side of their names on the roster sheet.

Chapter Thirteen
The Top of the Pyramid

Never forget that your students are teenagers or younger and are still developing into young adults. Teens need to feel comfortable, accepted and loved. When we understand this we are able to understand some of their behavior. We also need to remember not to take the things that teens do and say too seriously or personally. We should be aware that a teenager's mood swings take place every few seconds, or so it seems.

Comfort level is another way of saying stability. A teenager is going through a great deal of change in their life. Many people call middle school students "hormones in tennis shoes" for good reason. Stability is a part of the teen's comfort zone. The more stability that we are able to provide in the classroom, the better it is for our students. That means that we have to be consistent so that they know what to expect from day to day. If stability is missing from a student's life, they will seek it out or they will seek someone to bring it into their life. You may be the person that they seek. Most stability should come from their home life and their moms and dads.

When I was a teen I had a very secure and stable home life. My parents were and still are in love with each other. They made their relationship the first priority in their marriage and my brother and sisters benefited from their stable relationship. I never saw my parents have angry words towards each other. They always maintained a united front and when my father left the house he would always make it a point to kiss my mom goodbye in front of us. When we saw that take place we knew that all was well in our world. Even if everything broke loose in my world outside the home, I knew that once I returned home normality would be restored. This was my place of refuge and order.

If this world does not exist for your students they may look for it in your classroom. It is possible that your classroom will be the only stability they experience in a day or a week. You must communicate the stability in your own life as you communicate your expectations and consistently follow them. That way your students will know what to expect when they are in your class. I am not saying you should never throw a surprise or two into your teaching methods; I am saying that you should be consistent in your behavior and actions when dealing with your students. This will bring comfort and stability to your students.

Is there any doubt that students seek acceptance? Look at their clothing choices; for the most part they do not want to stand out. In some cases they do not want to be too successful and they do not want to look like failures. They want to be a part of the group and they want to be accepted for who they are. We should do our best neither to change them nor to judge them; even students who dress or act in outlandish ways are looking for us to accept them and their differences. Our students would like us to listen to them, to hear them out as they vent or express themselves. They may not want our advice. When a student comes to speak with you, you may want to ask them if they need your advice or just your ears to listen to them. This can be tough for a teacher as most of us want to fix problems and share our experience. We would like our students to avoid the mistakes we made or others have made. Yet in many cases we may need to allow them to make their choices and reap the consequences of those choices. After all, that is the way we learned and we have to give them the same opportunities.

I have attempted to make my classroom a place that accepts all. I have tried to create a kinder, gentler classroom, a classroom where students feel free to take educational risks and share opinions. A year after 9/11, I invited a former student, who happened to be Muslim, to discuss his faith with my students. I was not seeking to convert anyone; I was seeking an understanding for my students that the Muslim faith is not monolithic, that there are differences within groups that we have to account for. I want my students to take the risk of being wrong, to ask questions without the fear of ridicule. During the first few weeks of school I inform my students that there are no dumb questions, there are only unasked questions that have the effect of leaving one uninformed.

Conclusion

I enjoyed my 30 years at River Valley High School. I had outstanding students and very supportive parents. Our faculty and staff were professional and caring. I have not found any profession that provides the interactive opportunities such as those that are provided to a classroom teacher. But there comes a time to move on and accomplish other educational goals. This book is one, and there will be more goals to set and reach.

When I was active in the classroom I made it a point to treat and to teach my students as if they were my own children. I gave them the same attention, preparation and presentation that I would have given my own children if they had ever been my students. I am speaking of taking your respect for students one more step and that step is to love. I am not speaking of romantic love; I am speaking of kindness and compassion for a group of human beings who are going through some of the most challenging times of their lives. I have found that students often hunger for someone to show an interest in their lives, to show concern for what they are going through. They want to see you at their athletic contests and music performances. They want you to compliment their efforts. Your students will seek your approval and if you give it to them in a positive way they will reward you with their respect.

I know that my colleagues in the English department may discover a few errors in grammar as they read this collection of thoughts. They are my responsibility and if you wish you can email me and point them out. If there is a revision I will make sure to include the corrections. Does that work for you Mr. Hering and Mrs. Malley?

Also, I must recognize the finest Social Studies Department in the state of Ohio in Chris Danals, Ron Keiser, Randy Leach and the young man who replaced me in the classroom, Mark Bollinger.